Walks w
i
Yorkshire Dales
SWALEDALE

Mary Welsh

ᴬQUESTAGuide

© Mary Welsh 2005

ISBN 1 898808 21 X

Published by
Questa Publishing Ltd., PO Box 520, Bamber Bridge, Preston, Lancashire PR5 8LF
and printed by
Carnmor Print, 95/97 London Road, Preston, Lancashire PR1 4BA

Contents

Introduction

Swaledale

Entering Swaledale from its western end is like stepping back in time. One narrow road, the B6270, traverses the narrow valley bottom, through which the River Swale (meaning swift) flows. It is hedged in by steep-sided desolate fells, topped by broad lonely moors. Near Keld is the dramatic Kisdon gorge where, in glacial times, the river changed its course, isolating Kisdon Hill. Then the valley widens a little, allowing for walled meadows in which stand the characteristic field barns.

Beyond Keld, the Swale continues on it tempestuous way, tumbling in numerous spectacular waterfalls. It is joined by many equally lively side streams, Whitsundale Beck, East Gill, East Grain, Thwaite, Oxnop, Gunnerside and Barney. By the time the Swale reaches Grinton, joined by the Arkle, the valley has widened. The river, still fast flowing, passes through rich meadowland and past extensive lynchets.

At the entrance to the dale stands its capital, the fine town of Richmond, with its huge keep towering over a charming square and narrow alleys, known as wynds. Just outside the town's old wall lived the Grey Friars, and a beautiful tower of their monastery still stands. To the east of the town is Easby Abbey, where a branch of the Augustinian order enclosed land and bred sheep on a large scale. In the Middle Ages, much of Swaledale was controlled by the monasteries, which attained great wealth from wool and lead. The lead was used by abbeys and castles throughout Britain and France for roofing and gutters. To the west of Richmond, Marrick Priory housed nuns, who wore black habits.

John Wesley came to Swaledale in the middle of the 18th century. He preached to the miners, who appreciated a man they could understand. Many Methodist chapels were built, the money and often the labour coming from the miners themselves. They had a great wish to improve their education, as its shown by the existence of literary institutes at Muker, Gunnerside and Reeth.

Sheep farming is the main occupation of the scattered

communities, and the breed of sheep is named after the dale and pronounced 'Swa'dle'. The likeness of a Swaledale ram appears on the emblem of the National Park. Swaledale is part of the Yorkshire Dales National Park. It does not own the land and cannot make landowners do what they do not want to. It tries by education and advice to preserve the distinctive landscape made by generations of farmers, to preserve the scenery, the wildlife and the traditional buildings. It does not promote tourism, but seeks to help visitors enjoy the dale. It repairs footpaths and stiles.

You cannot fail to notice the stiles on all the walks in this book. Some are gap-stiles, formed by two well-placed slabs of stone. Many have small gates, on very strong springs, where the gap widens towards the top. Some are stone-stepped. All do their job well, providing access through the walls and keeping stock out. Overweight dogs will find them difficult.

The footpaths that criss-cross the dale make for ideal walking. Start with the easier walks and gradually work up to the more demanding ones when youngsters, for whom this book is compiled, are ready to tackle them. All the walks have interesting places to visit and young people will spot even more than are mentioned here. The views are magnificent. The wildlife reflects the soil and rock below. History, tragedy and comedy seem all about the dale. A gentle introduction to hill walking in such a glorious area will set children off on what could become a compulsive, lifelong and extremely healthy pastime.

1
Source of the River Swale

The River Swale comes into being where the Great Sleddale Beck merges with Birkdale Beck at the foot of forbidding moorland. To visit the confluence this walk starts from picturesque Keld, the highest village in Swaledale. Its grey cottages, built of fine closely grained stone from local quarries, cluster round the literary institute, the old school and the imposing United Reform Church.

Start: Park Lodge car park, Keld (GR893012), which lies at the end of the left turn at the foot of the village

Total distance: 9.8km (6 miles)

Height gain: 100m (330 feet)

Difficulty: Generally easy walking all the way, but the path to the start of the Swale and over the moor to Angram can be bleak on an overcast day. Choose a sunny day if possible, youngsters will enjoy it much more.

1 From the car park, return to the road and walk ahead to descend a walled track (signed Muker). Take the first left turn, an arm of the Pennine Way (PW). It is rough underfoot and quite steep as it drops down to a long footbridge over the River Swale. Cross and then pause in the lovely hollow to enjoy the first of the many stunning waterfalls seen on this walk.

2 Bear left for a few steps and then take a rough path, which winds right and climbs uphill, to pass through a gap in the wall above. Turn left to walk the PW to East Stonesdale farm, where the long-distance path bears right to continue to Tan Hill. Ignore this and go ahead here, remaining on the reinforced bridleway as it runs above the river valley, with extensive views into the upper dale.

3 Stride on along the pleasing track and follow it as it eventually descends to cross a bridge over the fine cascades of Currack Force. Remain on the track and continue climbing to a gate and then on to join a narrow fell road. Cross, and after a few steps uphill, take the signed footpath on the left. This

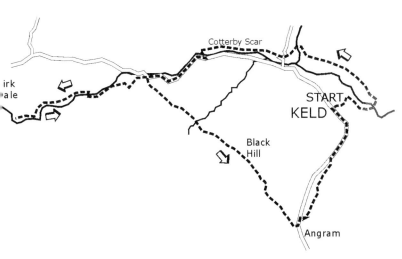

grassy way, above Cotterby Scar, traverses the moorland and runs high above the Swale. The stiled path is easy to follow but after rain becomes muddy in parts walk where others have walked before.

4 Follow the clear, stiled path to reach a waymark. Here turn sharp left to descend a track to cross Low Bridge. Turn right and walk the undulating B-road for half a mile to reach High Bridge. Do not cross but go on ahead along a short reinforced gated track (signed 'Footpath to Birkdale').

5 Beyond the gate, follow the waymark to walk to the left of the wall, with a small beck to your left. Go through a waymarked gate on your right, just before a barn. Then wind right to walk on beside a wall on your right below steepish slopes to your left. Once beyond several walls, go on ahead parallel with the Swale. Continue on until you can cross a gated bridge (1840) above the river.

6 Turn left and carry on the delightful way just above the river. Go through a gate and head on towards a farmhouse ahead. Pass through a gate and beyond the next gate, keep left of the dwelling. Head on along a wide grassy fenced way, and where the fencing ceases, to reach a track climbing right. Ignore this and turn left to wind round right, past a farmhouse and a large barn.

7 Carry on along a grand walled way. Just before it ends at the edge of the Birkdale Beck there is sometimes a large puddle to negotiate. Use the stones along the left side. Just before the Birkdale, walk a few steps left beside it to see the confluence of the two becks and the start of the River Swale. This is a magical moment.

8 Retrace your steps through the valley to High Bridge and the B6702. Here take, on the right, the gap-stile (signposted 'Angram, 1½ miles'). Follow a little path steeply uphill, bearing left towards the wall. After the short steep climb take the ladder-stile over the wall. Beyond, stroll the distinct path across the rough moorland to the next stile and then on to another stile. Once over this the long easy-to-follow path continues through heather to come to a reinforced track running along the edge of a gill through which flows Backburn Beck. Pause here and look for the widish path, on the opposite bank of the gill, climbing the slope ahead.

9 Cross and descend a faint path towards a grouse butt beside the beck. Step across at an easy place and climb straight uphill on the grassy trod you spotted earlier. It carries on over heather moorland to a stile in the wall ahead and then a rickety stile over a fence.

10 Follow the continuing airy path to cross more moorland to climb a stile over a fence and then a gated stile beyond. Walk on along the delightful shelf-like path, through heather, below Black Hill for 200m. Then take the narrow, easy-to-miss stile in wall on the right.

11 Turn half-left and soon wind right up a steadily climbing wide grassy track. Carry on to join a grassy track and bear left with it to go through a gate in the wall ahead. Head on over a rougher pasture to go through the next small gate in the wall. Walk on in the same general direction, gradually descending, to go through the next wall by a gate. Stroll on across the pasture to walk down beside the wall, now on your left, into the small hamlet of Angram.

12 Turn left, go past a phone box and on to a red metal gate on the opposite side of the road, just before the next dwelling. Descend the grassy sward to pass through a gap in the wall and then head on, descending a little, to go through a small gate in a wall corner. Continue beside the wall on your right to a small gate in the wall ahead. Then walk on, roughly parallel with the B-road, passing through several gated stiles. Cross

Aygill by a footbridge and carry on the stiled way. The last stile (9th) is up the slope and onto to the B-road. Turn right and stride on to the signposted right turn for Keld. Descend the narrow road and turn left at the bottom to reach the car park. Of course if you think the family will be too tired to tackle all the stiles, you could return to Keld by the road but they will probably enjoy locating the stiles and counting them.

Along the Way

Many **footpaths** radiate from Keld, taking you through glorious ancient woodland, beside the magnificent River Swale and over wild austere moorland, the haunt of curlew, dotterel, golden plover, snipe and skylark. Once the dale resounded with the sounds associated with lead mining and a legacy of this is a network of footpaths and packhorse trails much used by walkers. Today the dale resounds to the bleating of sheep and lambs.

Birds

The various calls of the curlew are quite distinctive and are recognised by most people. It is the largest of the wading birds, with long legs and a long curving bill. It spends the winter months on low ground. In early spring pairs arrive on the moors to breed, making a nest in a hollow lined with heather or grass. If you cross the moors to Angram in April watch for these lovely birds as they plane over the nest site. You might also spot or hear redshanks and oyster catchers which also nest on the moor.

But the real birds of the moorland are the red grouse. They remain all year feeding mainly on heather, above which their heads can often be seen. If you startle a grouse it flies low over the heather, making a loud whirring noise with its wings. Youngsters should watch out for these common birds and try to learn their 'goback, goback' calls.

---

3 hrs ✓

2
Kisdon Hill

In glacial times the River Swale changed its course, isolating Kisdon Hill. It is beside this lovely top, and then over it, that this walk takes you. The route starts at Muker, a village that sprang up to house lead miners. It is situated at the foot of Kisdon Hill and its clusters of stone cottages huddle together above the beck, which joins the River Swale just below the bridge to the east. The village has a Literary Institute, the old schoolhouse and St Mary's church, first built in 1580 to ease the demand for burials at Grinton. At that time Grinton church had the only consecrated ground in upper Swaldale.

Start: The pay-and-display car park at the east end of Muker (GR.912978).

Total distance: 9km (5½ miles)

Height gained: 130m (430 feet)

Difficulty: Moderate. Gentle ascents and descents. Very little road walking

1 From the car park at Muker, cross the bridge over Muker Beck and go on to pass in front of the literary institute. Turn right to climb a narrow road to go by the church. Just before a row of cottages, look for the signpost on the right. Continue along a ginnel to a gated stile. Beyond, a pleasing paved way takes you across hay meadows where you are asked to walk in single file.

2 The paved way passes through a number of gap-stiles, with the lonely valley unfolding ahead, and eventually brings you to steps down to the side of the River Swale. Here turn left and walk the narrow, but generally reinforced path, which is well waymarked. Keep to the raised flood bank, with the river to your right, and go on the stiled way.

3 Look for the small wooden gate in the wall on the right that leads you to lower ground nearer the river. As you reach a boundary wall ahead stretching towards the Swale, look for the easy-to-miss gap-stile, which takes you on ahead. Look right from here to see the awesome Swinner Gill on the other side of the valley and, high above it, Crackpot Hall.

4 Stride on through the dale along a short stretch of sunken

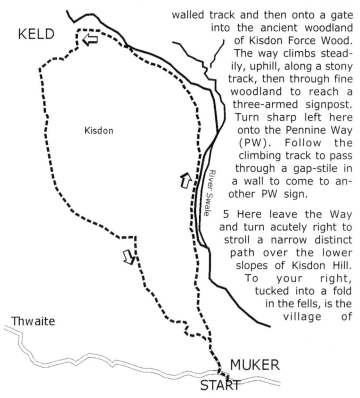

walled track and then onto a gate into the ancient woodland of Kisdon Force Wood. The way climbs steadily, uphill, along a stony track, then through fine woodland to reach a three-armed signpost. Turn sharp left here onto the Pennine Way (PW). Follow the climbing track to pass through a gap-stile in a wall to come to another PW sign.

5 Here leave the Way and turn acutely right to stroll a narrow distinct path over the lower slopes of Kisdon Hill. To your right, tucked into a fold in the fells, is the village of

Keld. The narrow way brings you parallel with a wall. As you near a stone sheepfold, on your right, the indistinct way moves away from it to pass through a sturdy gate onto a track.

6 Remain with the track as it gradually descends through gates, with an ever increasing, pleasing view of the hamlet of Thorns. At a T-junction of tracks, turn left to begin a steady climb along the bridleway, known as the corpse road, which takes you up onto Kisdon Hill.

As you go think of the medieval mourners who carried the coffins of their loved ones along this way. In 1580 a church was built at Muker, but until then the bearers took two days to journey the 12 miles from Keld to consecrated ground at St Andrew's, Grinton.

7 Stroll on, enjoying the glorious views down into Upper Swaledale. The way soon becomes a wide and grassy gated way, with regular signposts directing you towards Muker – here youngsters could seek out the route ahead of the adults.

8 At a division of tracks, take either way because both join up at a gate into a walled track. At the three-armed signpost, go on ahead and, 50m further on, at another three-armed signpost, continue down the signed bridleway to Muker, with a fine view of the gracefully curving Swale, the grassy way becomes reinforced and then winds left. It soon becomes metalled and from it you can see Muker. The track zigzags downhill, easing the gradient for all users and then, as a minor road, takes you into the village, where you turn left for the car park.

Along the Way
In many parts of England fields are ploughed and grass sown. The crop is then heavily fertilised. The grass is cut for silage several times throughout the summer. The fields become uniformly green and there are virtually no flowers. Meadows in the Dales are left to grow hay and have received little artificial fertiliser and so produce an abundance of flowers. The **hay meadows** about Muker are farmed by this traditional method and the result is a myriad wild flowers including yellow buttercups, followed by cow parsley, sweet cicely, meadow cranesbill, pink clover and the prolific mountain pansy. It should be remembered, on the walks in this book that hay is a vital crop for local farmers and they ask that walkers keep in single file along the paths through the meadows.

Commemorated on a plaque on Muker's old school is the story of the two naturalists **Richard and Cherry Kearton**. They walked to the school each day from the hamlet of Thwaite, where they were born in the 1860s. Richard was crippled as a result of an accident in childhood. As a young man he took what work he could get and managed to act as a beater for grouse shoots on the local moors. A publisher up from London, on a shoot, was amazed at the youths' knowledge and love of nature and offered him a job in his company. Richard accepted and was soon writing books on natural history and illustrating them with his own and his brothers photographs. They were the pioneers of nature photography. Until then photographers had mainly used dead or stuffed animals, but the Keartons spent many hours in the wild and produced photographs of wild life in a natural habitat.

3
Gunnerside to Ivelet and Oxnop Gill

*The old road from Calvert Houses, above Muker, to Gunnerside
has been superseded by the B6270 that runs throughout
Swaledale. This walk starts along the old road, from where
extensive views unfold. To reach the high-arched single-
spanned packhorse bridge over the River Swale you pass
through the hamlet of Ivelet, which stands on a limestone
terrace and once had its own inn. The B-road is then crossed and
quiet, steepish footpaths take you, through fine pastureland and
then moor, to explore a little of Oxnop Gill, a deeply cut side
valley of the Swale. The return is made along more footpaths
above the River Swale.*

Start: From the centre of Gunnerside (GR951982) (see walk
5 for alternative parking)

Total distance: 9km (5½ miles)

Height gain: 180m (590 feet)

Difficulty: The ascent and then the descent of Oxnop Gill is
quite steep but nothing that youngsters won't be able to
tackle and enjoy

1 Leave the centre of Gunnerside by taking the old road, which
heads west, directly opposite the Little Bridge. Continue on the
high level way, which is almost vehicle-free. The slopes of
Gunnerside Pasture rise up to your right and there is a pleasing
view down towards the Swale, with its walled pastures about
it. After one mile, follow the road as it descends steeply and
turns sharp left, crossing Grains Gill.

2 Where the old road winds right, carry on ahead to pass
Gunnerside Lodge. Descend the steeply curving road to Ivelet
and go on down the alder- and ash-fringed road as it swings
right, beside a lovely stretch of the Swale to your left. To the
right sandstone crags tower upwards and in spring this is a
mass of colourful wild flowers. Cross the river by the fine
packhorse bridge and look for the site of the coffin stone on the
right. Walk on up the lane to pass some delightful waterfalls on
the Oxnop Beck, as it races to join the Swale, to come to the
side of the B6270.

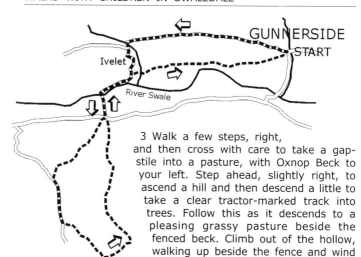

3 Walk a few steps, right, and then cross with care to take a gap-stile into a pasture, with Oxnop Beck to your left. Step ahead, slightly right, to ascend a hill and then descend a little to take a clear tractor-marked track into trees. Follow this as it descends to a pleasing grassy pasture beside the fenced beck. Climb out of the hollow, walking up beside the fence and wind round left to go through an easy-to-miss gate. Walk on up the slope to a stile, just ahead. Then begin the steep climb uphill, keeping along the rim of the gill. Pause as you go to look back, right, to see charming Little Oxnop.

4 At the top of the slope, climb a step-stile through the wall ahead. Walk along parallel with the woodland to your left and, where the trees end, stride across, half-left, over rather wet, rough ground to a signposted gate at the top of the pasture to join the fell road. Turn left and walk on for ¼ mile to take a signposted gap-stile on the left.

5 Head diagonally across a pasture to the bottom right corner and edge a tiny stream passing through a tumbledown wall. Walk on to cross the stream by a tractor bridge. Keep on the same diagonal to go over another tractor bridge across the little Stony Beck. Then follow the arm of the signpost to pass through a gate with a tall yellow-topped post. Turn left and walk up beside the wall, on the left, to pass through the second purpose-built gap to continue on the other side. A few steps along this side of the wall, go through a gate, wind left to cross the Oxnop by a footbridge. Beyond, walk right and then wind sharp left to climb a fine grassy slope. Half-way up, look for the stile, on the left, into a swathe of newly planted trees above the steep tree-clad slopes of the beck.

6 Enjoy the lovely path, its sides embroidered with primroses

in the spring. Note the signpost, directing you down and round right and then take the easy-to-miss gap-stile in the wall on your left, into bleak Spout Gill. Drop down the slope from the gap-stile and climb up a grassy path to a gate in the wall at the top of the gill. Pass above the two ends of descending walls, and, remaining on the same contour, head on until you can climb sturdy steps over a wall ahead. Beyond wind left and almost immediately, right, keeping beside the wall on your left. Carry on a good track to pass Gill Head farm and then along its access track to the fell road.

7 Turn left and descend for 100m to the first wall on your left. Beyond, take the signposted gap-stile on your left. Descend the slope parallel with the wall on your left and then swing, right, across the pasture, descending to a small gate in the next wall. Go on down to climb a stile over a fence, hidden by a fold in the hill, but located to the left of a small clump of trees. Then stride ahead to a gap-stile to the B-road.

8 Cross and walk a few steps left to turn right down the road to go over the packhorse bridge. Wind right and then left into Ivelet. Here take the right turn (signposted 'Footpath to Gunnerside'). At the end of the hamlet drop down a stepped path through magnificent vegetation to pause on the footbridge over the Shore Gill. Look left to see a glorious waterfall on the beck. Climb the steps out and then walk on towards Gunnerside using the easy-to-follow and most pleasing gated and stiled way over thirteen haymeadows. As you go, look right to see the hamlet of Satron, shadowed by Satron Side.

9 Carry on through the dwellings to the centre of the village.

Along the way

Ivelet Bridge spans the Swale at a wide part of the river. Until the 19th century ponies carried lead from local mines across the bridge.

Look for what might be the remains of the **corpse stone** on the far end of the parapet. Relays of bearers carried coffins in wicker baskets and laid them on the stone while resting. In 1580, a church was built at Muker, but until then the bearers took two days to journey the 12 miles from Keld to consecrated ground at St Andrew's, Grinton. A legend tells that a headless dog haunts the bridge and that bad luck comes to anyone who sees it.

4
Gunnerside Gill

The houses in the village of Gunnerside huddle close upon each other on either side of Gunnerside Beck. The small settlement, built of local stone with no intrusion of white painted walls, glows warmly in sunshine. It has a sloping green surrounded by cottages where once lived miners who worked the lead veins in the gills above the village.

This walk takes you up one of the longest and narrowest side valleys in Swaledale, where you pass much evidence of lead mining, the mines in the Gill being some of the most profitable in Swaledale. Most youngsters will enjoy seeing how people wrought a living here, 150 years ago, when lead mining was at its height. But they should be reminded to treat the relics with care. They should not explore the shafts or tunnels or go inside buildings which are, after century or so of having seen no maintenance, most unstable. Some of the relics are designated ancient monuments.

Start: In the centre of Gunnerside village (GR951983). Or if there is no space use the large verge just before the New Bridge, south of the village.

Total distance: 10km (6 miles)

Height gain: 201m (660 feet)

Difficulty: Moderate. Steady climb up the steep-sided Pennine valley

1 Take the footpath (signposted 'Gunnerside Gill'), between Little Bridge and Troutbeck House, opposite the King's Head, in the centre of the village. After 135m climb the steps on the right and walk on round the outside wall of a private house, once a school, into open fields. Then follow the waymarks to continue along the wooded beckside path into Birbeck Wood. Emerge from the trees by a gap-stile on the left and take another on the right, through the wall and continue beside it.

2 Go past the crushing floor of Sir Francis Mine and stroll along the clearly marked path to pass through the wall and carry on along a higher path, which used to serve the mine as a tramway. Look for the old buildings of the Dolly Lead level and its huge tip of spoil on the opposite side of the gill.

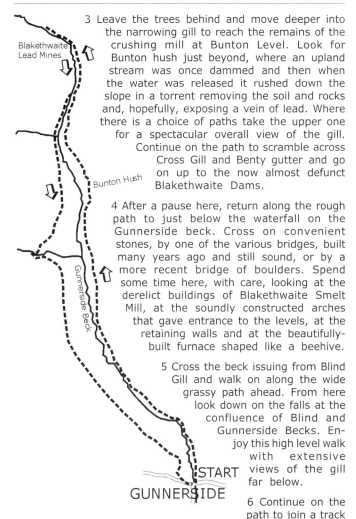

Blakethwaite
Lead Mines

Bunton Hush

Gunnerside Beck

START

GUNNERSIDE

3 Leave the trees behind and move deeper into the narrowing gill to reach the remains of the crushing mill at Bunton Level. Look for Bunton hush just beyond, where an upland stream was once dammed and then when the water was released it rushed down the slope in a torrent removing the soil and rocks and, hopefully, exposing a vein of lead. Where there is a choice of paths take the upper one for a spectacular overall view of the gill. Continue on the path to scramble across Cross Gill and Benty gutter and go on up to the now almost defunct Blakethwaite Dams.

4 After a pause here, return along the rough path to just below the waterfall on the Gunnerside beck. Cross on convenient stones, by one of the various bridges, built many years ago and still sound, or by a more recent bridge of boulders. Spend some time here, with care, looking at the derelict buildings of Blakethwaite Smelt Mill, at the soundly constructed arches that gave entrance to the levels, at the retaining walls and at the beautifully-built furnace shaped like a beehive.

5 Cross the beck issuing from Blind Gill and walk on along the wide grassy path ahead. From here look down on the falls at the confluence of Blind and Gunnerside Becks. En-joy this high level walk with extensive views of the gill far below.

6 Continue on the path to join a track by the magnificent waterfall (after rain) at the head of Botcher Gill. Walk on around the hairpin bend to pass through a gate and continue along the track to where there is another good view of the waterfall. Carry on along the easy way until it makes a long right turn. Here look for a cairn directing you

along an indistinct path (the track soon becomes clearer) in the direction of Gunnerside, which snuggles in a fold at the foot of the fell, its roof tops soon coming into view. On the edge of the village go through a little gate in a wall and drop down a short slope to the centre of the village.

Along the Way

At Gunnerside look for the fine **Methodist chapel** built in 1789 and rebuilt in 1866. Methodism flourished in the dale, where in the 19th century 2,000 men and boys worked the lead mines. A welcome but too infrequent visitor was John Wesley.

This exhilarating walk gives you a feeling for the endurance of the **lead miners** who walked to the Smelt Mills in all kinds of weather. One local legend tells of a miner who used to run the several miles home to prevent his wet clothes freezing on him. Work started early and tales are told of long rows of lights moving in the dark up the fells as the miners went to work, with candles in their hats to help them see their way. In summer many of them knitted as they wended their way up to the mines and hundreds of pairs of stockings were sold at the autumn fairs. During the middle of the 19th century, the life expectancy of miners was forty-six. Accidents claimed many lives, but most died from chest infections caused by breathing in dust. This damaged the lungs and brought about lead poisoning. To help improve their health miners were encouraged to keep a few sheep, hens and one or two cows on a small holding and to spend some time, out of doors, growing their own vegetables.

The Norsemen gave **Gunnerside** its name. It means gunnar's, or warrior's, pasture. Several of the local farmhouses are built in the style of Norse longhouses with continuous tiled roofs stretching over both the dwelling and the outbuildings. All the houses were built of local sandstone usually quarried nearby and roofed with thinner flagstones from the Yoredale series. These can be as much as a metre long, the size diminishing as the roof rises, each tile held in place by just one peg. Gunnerside is remarkable for the preservation of early field walls. Some of the fields are very small and the walls quite irregular.

5
Gunnerside to Low Row

This walk takes you along high, airy paths that traverse the slopes from where you have dramatic views down into Swaledale. Here the River Swale flows graciously, and in sunlight turns to a silver ribbon threading its way through the green pastures of the dale. Young people will enjoy the return walk, looking across the dale to see where they have walked earlier. There are many gap-stiles to seek out in the walls ahead and this gives youngsters the chance to develop their map reading skills by locating them.

Start: In the centre of the village of Gunnerside (GR951983)

If the parking area is full, use a large verge before New Bridge over the Swale, just south of Gunnerside.

Total distance: 7km (4½ miles)

Height gain: 50m (165 feet)

Difficulty: Easy, but if the Swale has come over its banks the track by which you return to Gunnerside can be muddy.

1 Leave the centre of the village by crossing the Little Bridge over Gunnerside Beck. Go past the King's Head and continue on past the small green. After the last house on the right, take the steep, gated, narrow road, left, up the slope. If the large metal gate is locked, use the small gate to the left. At the first zigzag, pursue the hedged track, climbing right. This soon reaches the open slopes with pleasing views up and down the dale.

2 Step across Stanley Gill and stride ahead along the walled way towards Lane Foot where an information board details the occupants of two ruined cottages over many years. Carry on up the walled way on a grassy trod. Where it winds left, up to the moor, and just beyond the first house over the wall on the left, take an easy-to-miss step-stile in the wall on your right.

3 Continue below two more houses (Heights) and then carry on ahead through a gap-stile and then a gap in the next wall. Go across the next pasture to take the next gap-stile and then climb a stile into the start of Rowleth Wood, where there is a 'Walkers welcome' sign. Keep to the right of the fence on a

slightly awkward path, passing young birch and rowan emerging from their protective sleeves.

4 Keep to the right of a continuing wall to follow a path, through mature woodland, which can be muddy after rain. Ash, sycamore and hazel grow about the slopes and through these slip many birds. Leave the trees by a gap-stile and go ahead on a steepish sloping pasture to pass through gaps in the next two walls. Strike half-left up the pasture to another gap and then take a very narrow gap-stile ahead and continue to a gate in the top corner. Beyond, walk below the barn of Smarber farm, then bear left up beside the barn on a short cobbled way. Pass through a gate onto a reinforced track and walk right.

5 Where the track swings sharp left, cross a grassy tractor bridge over a lively beck. Bear right to pass through a farm gate to join a wide grassy track. Walk below Smarber Cottage and steadily descend. Go through the next gate and continue gently down and into trees. Cross a fine footbridge over a dancing beck, which tumbles in three white-topped falls hidden

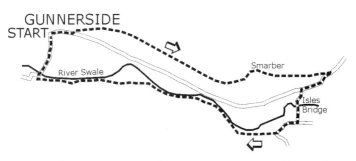

in a leafy gill. Stride on along a sometimes muddy track to reach the edge of Low Row, a hamlet which sprawls along the B6270.

6 Drop down a short grassy slope to a seat just above the B-road. Turn right and follow the signpost directing you along a bridleway that keeps parallel with the road. Just beyond the chapel, wind left, with the beck to your right, to join the B-road. Cross and continue on along the verge to take the left turn for Crackpot. Go over Isles Bridge, above the Swale, and walk on to the T-junction, where you turn right to walk on along a 'No through road' (Dubbing Garth Lane). Stroll on where the tarmac ceases to pass Dubbing Garth cottage. At a Y-junction

keep to the right branch and walk on the sometimes rough track, where it has been washed out by the River Swale. For 1½ miles, the lane keeps mainly parallel with the river, then it moves away from the river and continues on through pastures. Just before it reaches the B6270 leave the track, right, for a few steps, to a gate in the corner and descend steps to the B-road and turn right to return to your starting point.

Along the Way

Limekilns Throughout the Dales you come upon limekilns, set against a hillside. Inside is a shaft, tapering towards the top. At the bottom of the kiln, peat, wood and sometimes coal was used to ignite lumps of limestone. Workers loaded more limestone into the kiln from the top, reaching it by a ramp. The lime, after firing, was extracted from the base. Burnt lime was needed as a fertiliser to reduce the acidity of soil, grazing animals needed its calcium and it was also used, mixed with water and sand, in mortars and plasters for houses.

Lime-rich soils These result in good grassland. Ash is the dominant tee, accompanied by yew, hazel, beech, lime, holly, pine, rowan, birch, hawthorn, hornbeam and blackthorn; many of the latter being found in Rowleth Wood. Oak, alder and sycamore grow nearer the valley bottom.

Low Row and **Feetham** are now one long village. Many of the houses were built for miners. Thomas Armstrong the novelist lived here, and in 1952 he published 'Adam Brunskill', in which he well describes the lead mines of earlier times.

In Norman times large tracts of Swaledale were reserved as **hunting forest** and would have been full of deer, boars, wolves, hares, otters, badgers and foxes. With the growth of the population through the centuries the area changed from a wild environment to a farming one, driving away many animals. With the growth of the mining industry and the cutting down of trees for fuel the habitat for wild animals became even more restricted. So it is a great pleasure to walk through Rowleth Wood where the local community has improved the stiles and planted many more trees on what was once rough pasture.

✓ 2hrs 40 min

6

Reeth to Grinton

*There is much of interest on this walk, which youngsters will
enjoy: a high moorland track with dramatic views into the upper
dale; a delightful riverside stroll; three pleasing villages, one
with a museum; Anglo-Saxon strip lynchets and a church with
traces of Norman architecture. Healaugh, half-way along the
walk, once housed dozens of lead miners in newly built cottages
and where the walk nears its end, at Grinton, you'll be in the
parish that was once the largest in Yorkshire, stretching from
near Richmond to Keld. Here the countryside is wooded and
softer and the village is known as the 'green settlement'.*

Start: Reeth village green (GR038993)
Total distance: 9km (5½ miles)
Height gained: 290m (970 feet)
Difficulty: Generally easy walking

1 Leave the large green at Reeth and turn left into Silver Street
(B6270) to walk in front of the Buck Hotel. Continue past the
fire station and climb a little way up the hill. Take a narrow
walled track on your right, signposted Skelgate Lane. Follow
this steadily climbing way, walled and then tree-lined, for more
than ½ mile, pausing on your way to enjoy views of austere
Fremington Edge and down to Reeth.

2 Pass through a gate on to the open moor and continue ahead
with the wall to your left. Stride on past Riddings Farm, over
the wall on your left, and go on to walk beneath Calver Hill
(420m) on your right. Carry on beside the dark gritstone wall
and pause occasionally to peer over at the fascinating field
patterns that quilt Harkerside on the far side of the valley. Look
out for walled fields shaped like a cup and a jug no-one knows
the reason!

3 Soon the track becomes solidly reinforced and you should
walk this good way for nearly a mile, over the high moorland,
with incredible views through the dale. Follow it as it begins to
descend (waymarked) to pass a cottage named Moorcock.
Wind down left to join a narrow road and walk sharply left.
Follow it as it drops steeply to the charming village of
Healaugh. Turn left to walk the narrow street (B6270), which

is bordered by pretty cottages and houses.

4 Turn right beyond Manor House, almost the last house on the right, to follow a grassy track (signposted 'Grinton and Reeth via Riverside'). Then stride on beside the wall on your left to the side of the alder-lined River Swale. Turn left and begin the lovely stiled way beside the fast-flowing water. Where the path divides, keep right along the riverside path. Go over a small plank bridge and carry on to cross the fine suspension bridge, called a swing bridge by local people. It has a very interesting information board beside it. Pause here and look back across the river to see the cultivation terraces on the slopes below Reeth School.

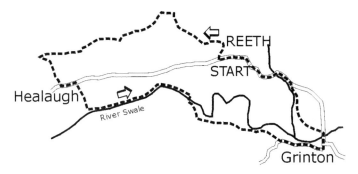

5 Turn left and walk on parallel with the river and then, when it makes a large curve and there are huge shingle beds, continue on, a little way from it. Look for the conical hill on the right, named a 'tumulus' (an ancient burial site) on maps. As you go look for traces of an earthwork running down the slopes, west of Dyke House farm. Stroll on the clear path, with glimpses of the river to your left. After locating and climbing a stile tucked into the corner of the fence, to your left, wind round a fallen tree, moving left into the field and then curving back into the hedge-lined path. Stroll on the glorious way to arrive at a narrow metalled lane. Turn left and walk into Grinton.

6 If you wish to visit the church, known as the 'Cathedral of the Dale', go through a gate on the left into the churchyard. The beautifully proportioned church is a delight. It has a lofty barn roof. Look for the leper squint and a copy of Birkett's New Testament in a glass-topped cabinet.

7 Leave the churchyard by the far-left gate and turn right. Go past a charming house with a glorious garden and carry on ahead to cross the fine arched bridge over the Swale. Just before the end of the bridge, don't miss the gated steps down into a meadow, on the left. Here youngsters might look back to see the different shaped arches and work out a reason for this. Walk along the path across the meadow and to the right you might spot more traces of the earthwork. Follow the waymarked path as it winds steadily right. Pass through a gate beside the outbuildings of what was once a corn mill and later supplied electricity for the village. Walk the path beside the River Arkle to join the B6270 and turn left. Cross Reeth Bridge over the river and continue uphill towards the green at Reeth.

Along the Way

Lynchets: Strip lynchets look like long gigantic grassy steps. They were agricultural terraces, created by our Anglo-Saxon ancestors, for growing crops in the 6th and 7th centuries. Crops were grown on the strips between the ridges. Ploughing was carried out using teams of oxen pulling heavy wooden ploughs the width of the team determined the width of the lynchet.

Walled enclosures: By the suspension bridge you can see the small enclosures stretching up the hillsides, including the cup and jug fields referred to in the walk. These walls extend to the riverside so that every owner had access to water and a share of the richer soil lower down.

Sheep are undemanding animals. They will nibble happily at anything in a pasture and graze it to the ground. They have to be hardy enough to withstand the cold and wet winter. Apart from the Herdwick, the Swaledale is the hardiest of all British sheep. It is identified by a fine set of spiral horns and a black face about a white nose. It has an important role as a crossing breed, the mother of such hybrids as the Mule and the Masham. Many of the great abbeys of Yorkshire grew rich from the wool clipped from their great flocks.

7

Reeth, Fremington Edge and Arkle Beck

Reeth, known as the small capital of Swaledale, lies at the foot of the side valley of Arkengarthdale. It has many sturdy houses, pretty cottages and welcoming shops, which stand around the peaceful spacious green. There is little to remind you that it was once the centre of a vast lead mining area.

Overlooking the village is the forbidding wall of Fremington Edge, which now shows a mainly grassy face to the village. But around hidden corners and close beside the paths are gullies, spoil heaps, hushes and quarries, created by the miners, now softened by low growing plants. The climb to the Edge will be quite a challenge for youngsters. Take lots of pauses and set targets as you climb, for example, 'When we reach the white cottage let's pause for an apple'.

Start: Reeth: By the shops at the west side of the large sloping village green (GR038993)

Total Distance: 10.5km (6½ miles)

Height gain: 230m (690 feet)

Difficulty: Steep climb at the start and then a lovely stroll along the Edge. The descent is steep, too, but all the route is well graded. Pleasing airy walk and a delightful return along the riverside

1 Descend the green and go on down the narrow Richmond Road. Carry on winding left to cross Arkle Beck by the bridge built in 1773 by the famous bridge master, John Carr of York. It replaced one destroyed two years earlier by a great flood that also destroyed bridges over the Swale at Richmond and Downholme.

2 Walk on from the bridge to take, on the left, a signposted squeeze-stile. Turn left and stroll beside the wall on your left to a gate. Beyond, go on past a barn to a gated stile. Then bear slightly right and walk on to climb a tree-clad hillock. Pass through a waymarked stile in the wall on the right. Go straight ahead up over a pasture to a gap-stile and then ahead again, keeping to the left of a barn to the next gap-stile. (Notice this one for your return.)

ᴗ Now begin your climb of the slopes, taking a grassy trod that ascends ahead. After about 100m, watch for the grassy way bearing right, and upward. Head towards the tops of several larches, which you can soon see above the slope. Below these trees stands a cottage, named White House on maps. Go through a gated stile in the top right wall corner, just above the cottage.

Storthwaite Hall

Fremington Edge

Castle Farm

REETH
START

4 At the footpath signpost, standing forlornly beside a reinforced track, walk left for a few yards and then take another grassy trod on the right. Follow this steadily up the slope along the edge of a gully. Away to the right you can see the old chert quarries where hard flint was obtained. It was crushed to a powder used in making china and pottery.

5 Follow the faint trod upwards to pass through a derelict wall to arrive on the flat top of the Edge – with the climbing finished. Turn left and walk beside the wall, now on your left, to a gap-stile in the wall corner, with a ladder-stile immediately beyond it. Climb this to walk left along Fremington Edge still with the wall to your left. The wide flat grassy way enables you to stride out and enjoy the magnificent views into Arkengarthdale and Swaledale. To your right, hiding the scars of 18th- and 19th-century dereliction, grow acres and acres of heather, a paradise for bees, grouse, green plovers and curlews.

6 Continue on the high level way for 1¾ miles to where the long straight wall turns right for a metre or so, before continuing on ahead. Here leave the Edge, left, passing through a gateway, to begin your descent. Follow the path right, west, as it leads towards some spoil heaps and soon becomes clearly cairned and then waymarked with posts. Before you wind left through more spoil, look across the Slei Gill to see the huge North Rake hush, where miners exposed veins of lead by damming back, then releasing a torrent of water.

7 The waymarking takes you safely and easily down the steep way, but pause as you go to look for the tiny hamlet of Booze set among trees. As you near the valley bottom, look ahead to see a tall post by a wall, with a waymark on its top, denoting the gate where you go through the wall. Stay with the wall on the right to pass a cottage, on your right, and join a farm track. Turn left and stroll on to pass a farmhouse and outbuildings. Beyond, a signposted grassy track takes you across two meadows, and brings you close to the lovely Arkle Beck and a footbridge. Do not cross.

8 Enter a small wood by a gate and go on to take the path to the right. Follow the blobs of paint on trees. Cross an easy-to-miss stile on your left and continue parallel with a ditch and the Arkle Beck until you reach a two-armed signpost. Here take the direction for Reeth, walking slightly right to a stile (blobs of paint guide you). Go on by the wall on the right to pass behind Castle House farmhouse.

9 Turn right into a walled track and then left to continue on the obvious waymarked path. Go past a derelict cottage on your left. As you enter more woodland you soon come close to the Arkle. Press on to a signpost directing you along a good terraced track through the glorious deciduous trees. Follow this gated way for just over ¼ mile until you reach the gap-stile in the wall, on your right, which you passed through (and noted) to start your climb up to the Edge.

10 Beyond, retrace your outward route – descend right of a barn, go through two stiles, turn left and cross the field to take another stile. Beyond, keep to the right hand wall over two fields, to the stile to the left of the bridge over the Arkle. Turn right to return to Reeth.

Along the Way

In monastic times, Rievaulx Abbey held the lead mining rights in Swaledale. By the 18th century, several thousand tons were produced annually, the industry reaching its peak in the early 19th century. It failed in the second half of the century as a result of cheap imports. Hand-in-hand with lead mining went knitting. By the beginning of the 19th century, Reeth knitters were making thousands of pairs of stockings every year - but this success was not enough to save jobless miners and their families from having to move away to other counties or abroad when the mining failed.

8

2hᵣₛ 50mₙₛ

Marrick to High Fremington

Marrick is a quiet brownstone hamlet high on the slopes above the Swale. When the old road from Richmond passed through it to Reeth, it was a much more important and busy place. Its chapel and church are now dwelling houses. It has a tiny triangular green with a seat, and is reached by narrow roads over spacious rolling pastures, because this is the area where Swaledale begins to widen and its contours become softer.

Little remains of Marrick Priory. It has a 12th-century house and a 13th-century tower, built for the Benedictine nuns. It is now part of a working farm and also an outdoor centre. The nuns who one would imagine had a quiet contemplative life, in this remote part of Swaledale, did have problems. They had disputes with the Prior of Bridlington who insisted that he had the right to grind his corn in their mill because Mill Dam was on his land.

Start: Reeth village green (GR038993)

Total distance: 9km (5½ miles)

Height gain: 159m (522 feet)

Difficulty: Easy walking all the way. Some road walking. Plenty of mud around farm gates after rain

1 Descend from the green at Reeth by the Richmond Road and carry on, left, to cross the bridge over Arkle Beck and then walk on for approximately 140m. Go through the gate on the right side of the road (signposted 'Grinton'), and walk beside the beck. Go through a gate and wind right with the track and continue beside a row of posts on your left. Bear round left, as directed by the waymarker and walk on to take steps to a gap-stile onto Grinton Bridge. Cross the road and descend to the riverside to walk the delightful stiled footpath until it leads you up a slope to a stile onto a tarmac road.

2 Turn right and walk towards the farm, which incorporates Marrick Priory. Just beyond the farm turn right onto a wide tarmac drive and descend a little to visit the chapel (within the outdoor centre) and view the remains of the Priory.

3 Return to the road, turn right, cross a cattle grid and turn left through a gate to climb a green path to a gate into Steps Wood. Follow the splendid flagged way, known as the Nuns Causey, up through glorious ash woodland. In spring the way is lined with colourful flowers. Emerge from the trees by a gate and pause to enjoy the pleasing view down to the Swale. Bear half-left, ignore a gap-stile on the right and walk up beside the wall, on your right. Pass through a farm gate and go on along the metalled way into the hamlet of Marrick, passing the old Wesleyan Chapel on the way.

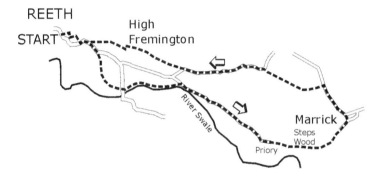

4 At the Y-junction, turn left and continue uphill past the small green, with a seat, on your right, and then a farm on your left. Press on gently uphill before descending a little to take an easy-to-miss stile, on your left, before the next wall you can see. Ascend beside the wall to pass through another easy-to-miss gated stile in the wall, which is faintly marked with yellow paint. Walk on up beside the wall, now on your left. Carry on the stiled way. From the top of the slope, on a Friday, you might spot the market stalls on the green at Reeth. Go on to a gate to the road and dawdle on, left.

5 Carry on down the road. Look right to see a well-preserved limekiln and then on, to pass the entrance to The Hagg. Descend through ash woodland. Ignore the footpath on the left and after ¾ mile along this lovely lane, where the road bends left, pass through the stile on the right, signposted Fremington.

6 Walk ahead, with the bleak slopes of Fremington Edge towering to your right, to a corner stile and then walk on beside

the wall on your right. Stride ahead along the stiled and gated way, with the now pleasingly wooded slopes of the Edge above. Cross a narrow track and stride along a partly walled and hedged path to join a metalled lane. Turn left and in a few steps take the lane on the right towards Reeth. (First you might like to make a detour through the small village with charming houses and lovely gardens.)

7 Where the lane turns left and descends to the main road, go ahead on a track. Beyond the gate, keep beside the wall on your left and follow it through a wall gap, then a stile. Walk on to take a gap-stile through the wall. Strike diagonally across the pasture to go through a gate and, beyond, to the road.

8 Cross Arkle Bridge and take the signposted track, a few steps along on the left. Follow the footpath as it soon winds, left, under the road bridge. Just beyond, follow the waymarks along a narrow grassy trod, beside the tree-lined Arkle, to take the first left, a fenced and grassy way between two fields. Climb the steepish, narrow walled path, which leads to a cobbled track. Turn right and ascend for several metres where, to the right is the cobbled way to the Swaledale Museum which you might wish to visit. The museum depicts the past life styles of the people who inhabited the Dales. Displays include lead mining, farming, village life and traditions (entrance fee). Or turn left to reach the village green.

Along the way

A story is told of **Isabella Beaufort**, who was courted by Henry VIII. She did not return his affection and sought sanctuary at Marrick Priory. The nuns kept her hidden for four years, but allowed her to write to her sweetheart, Edward Herbert. When Henry dissolved the priories and monasteries the nuns had to leave, but Isabella married Edward and they lived happily ever after in Somerset.

The **walls** of Swaledale were built to enclose grazing land. The field barns, one for two or three fields, were used to store hay and house cattle during the winter. The cows spent the summer in the meadows and then in November were moved into the barns, four or five to each stall. Twice a day the farmer would visit all his barns to feed the cattle from the stored hay and to milk them. He would also remove the dung that dropped into a channel. Today cattle are housed near the farm and the barns are rarely used.

9
Willance's Leap

*Attempt this walk when you are sure the children are ready for a
longer walk. There is a steady but well-contoured climb all the
way to Whitcliffe Scar. Then the path along the top of the scar is
sheer joy, with tremendous views ahead and in retrospect.
Willance's Leap is a great place for a picnic, but younger children
will have to be careful near the edge of the steep slopes.*

Start: At the car park on the south side of Reeth Road
A6108, just under a mile, west, from Richmond and close to
the River Swale and the Richmond caravan site (GR157008)

Total distance: 9.5km (6 miles)

Height gain: 210m (693 feet)

Difficulty: Steady climbing on the outward route but nearly
all downhill, and then level walking, on the return

1 From the car park beside the River Swale, go through a gap
in the barrier at the far (west) side of the car park. Ignore any
continuing tracks and walk right to a widish track, which, in a
few steps, climbs several concrete steps to the A-road.

2 Cross the road with care and walk left to take, a short way
along, a reinforced signposted track on the right. (Opposite to
this signpost is one that will take you back to the car park, but
it is a very rough path and not easy to locate from its foot.)
Stride the hedged concrete track and, after 200m, take the
pleasing green lane, hedged on both sides, which climbs right,
steeply at first and then more easily.

3 Follow the lane as it winds right and levels, with fine views
towards the North York Moors. At the dwelling, Low Leases, the
track bears left and ascends gently to a narrow tarmac lane.
Turn left and stroll on. Stand by the seat and enjoy the view,
over Richmond, that Alfred Wainwright so admired when he
walked his Coast to Coast Walk. Go on past Whitcliffe farm to
walk a private road, where you are asked to remain on the
right-of-way. Beyond a gate across the track at High Leases,
take the well-signposted stile on the right. Stride straight up
the slope to a small marker post and then turn left to walk a
rising path over the lovely down-like pasture. This brings you
to two stiles at a wall corner, which you climb.

4 Turn left and walk alongside the boundary on your left to a stile. Here a decision has to be made, whether to climb it or not! The path, going on right, is clear along the outside of the wire, but in places there are some serious drops down the scar. The maps show that the path continues inside the fence and there are stiles over boundary walls except at one place, at the time of writing, where the stile has collapsed on the ground and you will need to step over a wire fence. Here the

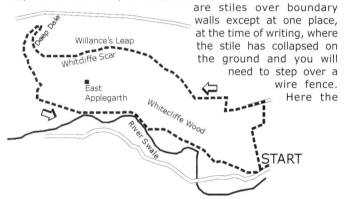

Deep Dale

Willance's Leap

Whitdiffe Scar

East Applegarth

Whitecliffe Wood

River Swale

START

barbed wire has been wound back. This second option is preferable if you have young children.

5 Continue along whichever path you have chosen, to climb the appropriate stiles on to a grassy track beside a small Sitka spruce plantation, on your right. The next stile leads out onto open pasture, with the boundary to your left. A short way along, go through an iron kissing-gate to a grassy flat to view the monument and memorial plaque to Robert Willance. There is a seat against the wall under a shady ash. Here is the place to pause and enjoy the glorious views but young children will need to warned of taking care on the slopes.

6 Then go on along the path, with the wall to your right. Just before it reaches the next stile small children will need to be under control; older children will enjoy it. Beyond the stile, follow the path up a slope and follow the lovely high way, with glorious view ahead. The path winds right, with a wall, around the rim of Deep Dale, and brings you to a little grassy path on the left just before a small TV booster. Descend the path to a narrow road, where you turn left.

7 The road descends steeply, with fine limestone buttresses, on the scar to your left. To the right, lofty trees shade steep grassy slopes. In spring these support vast numbers of

cowslips, intermingled with early purple orchids. Carry on downhill until you reach a cattle grid. Here you are directed right to a gated stile into a pasture. Drop down the slope to a stile on your left (part of the Coast to Coast trail). Do not climb the stile but walk right to waymark, then drop down the slope to a stile under a huge sycamore. This short curving way avoids Low Applegarth farm.

8 Beyond, go through a gate, on the left, with a yellow post. Then keep on the stiled way. Youngsters will enjoy using the map to locate these, or they might like to stand by one stile and spot the next one before moving on. The way leads to the side of a lovely stretch of the River Swale. Then the path cuts across the pasture as the river makes a large bend. Here look up on the top of the scar to see the monument to Robert Willance.

9 Climb the stile beside a small stream and then head over towards the side of the Swale once more where, in May, dozens of sand martins nest in the banking. Look left to enjoy the magnificent woodland, which stretches right down the steep scar above which you walked. A few steps on you have a choice of routes. You can either cut across the pasture and take a stile into Whitcliffe Wood and walk on, or continue round by the river to join a track, which soon unites with the one through the woodland.

10 Climb gently through the trees, a lovely bluebell woodland in spring. Just before a gate across the track, take the very well-signposted diversion, that keeps you to the left side of Lowenthwaite farm. Once past you join, by a stile, the track once more. The hedged way continues and passes a dwelling and then the bottom of the green lane taken at the outset of the walk. Stroll on to the A-road, turn left and walk a few steps to cross to the concrete steps to return to the car park.

Along the way

Robert Willance lived and died at 24 Frenchgate in Richmond. One day, in 1606, while he was hunting on horseback on Whitcliffe Scar, the mist came down. He spurred his horse into hurrying home and the mare leapt over the scar, plunging 62m (200 feet). Sadly the horse was killed but, miraculously, Robert survived, losing only his leg. He became an alderman of the town in 1608 and in gratitude for his survival presented a chalice to the corporation. He died in 1616 and was buried in the churchyard of St Mary, Frenchgate. Walkers should not attempt this walk if the scar is in mist.

10
Richmond to Easby Abbey

At the foot of Swaledale stands the town of Richmond, full of architectural splendour. It has a huge cobbled, horseshoe-shaped market place at the centre of which stands the chapel of Holy Trinity, founded in or about 1135. A huge obelisk rears upwards, built on the site of a medieval cross. Towering over the pleasing houses and shops that surround the market place, is the great Norman keep of the castle built by Alan Rufus in 1071 to protect himself from the Saxons. It was built on precipitous crags rising from the River Swale. In 1782, Castle Walk was constructed as a fashionable Georgian promenade to take advantage of the splendid views. After this delightful short walk, leave time to explore the magical corners of Richmond, the capital of Swaledale; all the family will enjoy it.

Start: Market Square, Richmond (GR172008). If there is no space available, use the Nuns Close car park, off Hurgill Road (GR168012). Leave by the pedestrian exit and cross the A-road, turn left and take the first right, Rosemary Lane, and then Finkle Street, to reach Market Square.

Total distance: 4km (2½ miles)

Height gain: 30m (100 feet)

Difficulty: Easy walking except for the steepish climb up from the river

1 Leave the Market Place by Tower Street, along the side of the Town Hall Hotel. Then wind slightly left along a charming street until you can descend steps. Turn right and walk downhill to bear left into Riverside Road. A short way along, drop right down a reinforced track, with fine parkland to your right running down and then across to the side of the River Swale. From the continuing footpath you have a good view of the fine arched gritstone bridge over the Swale.

2 Cross Station Road and go ahead along Lombards Wynd. Turn right along Easby Low Road and then go on the continuing unsurfaced lane, signposted for Easby Abbey. Stroll through the delightful woodland of Clink Bank and at the crest of the slope, look back for a fine view of Richmond. Then descend

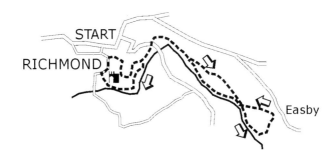

gently to a Y-junction of paths.

3 Immediately ahead is the Drummer Boy Stone, a stone slab standing on a stone plinth with an interesting plaque. After a pause to ponder on the poignancy of the legend on the stone, go on, keeping right of the memorial, along the lovely hedged path for half a mile. Just before the gate at the end of the path, notice the steps on the right, down to the side of the Swale, which you take on your return.

4 Beyond the gate, walk on along the waymarked fenced edge of the pasture, above shallow cliffs, with the Swale down right. Carry on to pass through a kissing-gate and wind on by a wall on your left, passing charming Abbey Mill, a former corn mill. Stride on to enter the gate on your left into the environs of Easby Abbey where you will wish to explore the extensive ruins.

5 Press on along the lane to visit the lovely little church of St Agatha of Sicily; again you will wish to pause here. Then continue along the lane as it winds left and begins to climb. A short way uphill, take the signposted pleasing track, leading left. A short way along is a waymarked stile, on the left, which you also take. From both of these tracks there is a splendid view of the abbey ruins in their entirety.

6 Carry on across a pasture to the kissing-gate into woodland. Beyond, descend the steps down to the side of the Swale and continue through fine deciduous woodland. Eventually the path leaves the trees and continues on to join the track at the foot of Clink Bank close to the Drummer Boy Stone. Stroll on ahead, in the direction of Richmond, and continue to walk left along Lombards Wynd and over Station Road. Then cross the

grass to walk beside the Swale once more. Follow the river until you come within sight and sound of the fine falls on the Swale and then go into a small car park. Turn right and climb the road to the bottom of the steps, taken earlier.

7 Here turn acute left to promenade along Castle Walk. This takes you below the castle walls, with a sheer drop (fenced) to the Swale. The views are splendid, with picturesque Green Bridge far below. As you continue round you can see Culloden Tower, built in 1746 by John Yorke to mark the Duke of Cumberland[1]s defeat of Bonnie Prince Charlie.

8 Carry on along the walk to where you have parked.

Along the way

The Drummer Boy was lowered, by soldiers, below the obelisk in the market place and told to find his way along underground passages believed to exist between the Castle and Easby Abbey. Legend has it that the boy was never seen again but occasionally people say they have heard a drum beat. The slab, seen on the walk, marks the last place the soldiers heard the drum.

Easby Abbey was founded in 1155 by Roald, Constable of Richmond Castle. In the time of Edward III, it came into the possession of the Scropes, lords of Bolton. The abbey suffered from frequent Scottish raids during the Middle Ages. Ironically, great damage was caused in 1346 when the English army was billeted nearby on its way to the battle of Neville's Cross. In the late 1530s, Henry VIII dissolved all monasteries. The ruins are a grand place for youngsters to explore but they are asked not to climb on the walls.

The **Church of St Agatha**, a Sicilian saint martyred by the Romans in the 3rd century AD, is a Norman foundation. Enjoy its splendid 14th century porch. In the chancel is a large piscina and three trefoiled stone seats. Look for the font dating from about AD 1100. It is large enough for a small child to be immersed, as was the practice in earlier years. Behind it is the wall bench that offered the only seating in the medieval period when pews were rarely used. Such provision gave rise to the saying 'the weak go to the wall'. Its greatest treasure is perhaps the wonderful 13th-century wall paintings. These were plastered over for several centuries and restored in 1994. Youngsters will enjoy trying to identify the biblical pictures.

Other titles by
QUESTA PUBLISHING

WALKS WITH CHILDREN

LAKE DISTRICT

Borrowdale
Buttermere and the Vale of Lorton
Around Coniston
Keswick and the Newlands Valley
Around Ambleside and Grasmere
Ullswater
Around Kendal
Around Windermere
South Lakeland

YORKSHIRE DALES
Wharfedale

PEAK DISTRICT
Dark Peak

also

SHORT WALKS IN THE EDEN VALLEY & NORTH PENNINES

All QUESTA title
are available from
PO BOX 520, BAMBER BRIDGE, PRESTON,
LANCASHIRE PR5 8LF

or by FAX to
0870 138 8888

Website: www.questapublishing.co.uk